Thomas & Nanette KINKADE
with LARRY LIBBY

THE Many Loves OF *Christmas*

Multnomah Gifts™
Multnomah® Publishers *Sisters, Oregon*

THE MANY LOVES OF CHRISTMAS
published by Multnomah Gifts, a division of Multnomah® Publishers, Inc.
Text © 2003 by Thomas and Nanette Kinkade
Featuring artwork by Thomas Kinkade © 2003 by Thomas Kinkade,
Media Arts Group, Inc., Morgan Hill, CA

International Standard Book Number: 1-59052-090-4

Design by Koechel Peterson & Associates, Minneapolis, Minnesota

Unless otherwise indicated, Scripture quotations are taken from:
The Holy Bible, New International Version© 1973, 1984 by International
Bible Society, used by permission of Zondervan Publishing House
Other Scripture quotations:
The Holy Bible, New King James Version (NKJV).
© 1982 by Thomas Nelson, Inc. Used by permission.
Holy Bible, New Living Translation (NLT)
© 1996. Used by permission of Tyndale House Publishers, Inc.
All rights reserved.

Printed in China

For Information:
MULTNOMAH PUBLISHERS, INC. • P.O. BOX 1720
SISTERS, OR 97759

Library of Congress Cataloging-in-Publication Data
Kinkade, Thomas, 1958-
    The many loves of Christmas / by Thomas and Nanette Kinkade with Larry Libby.
        p. cm.
    ISBN 1-59052-090-4
1. Christmas—California. 2. Christmas in art. 3. Jesus Christ—Nativity. I. Kinkade, Nanette.
II. Libby, Larry. III. Title.
    GT4986.C2K55 2003
    263'.915—dc21

                        2003005738

        03 04 05 06 07 08 09—10 9 8 7 6 5 4 3 2 1 0

Table OF *Contents*

6
The Christmas Pool

10
The Courts of the Lord

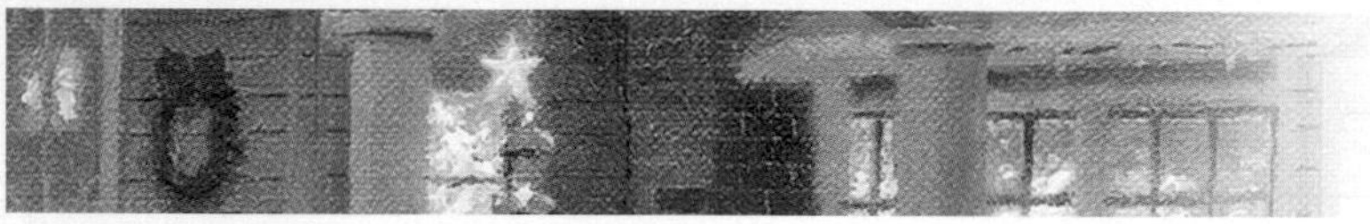

16
First Christmas

22
"Happy Birthday, Jesus!"

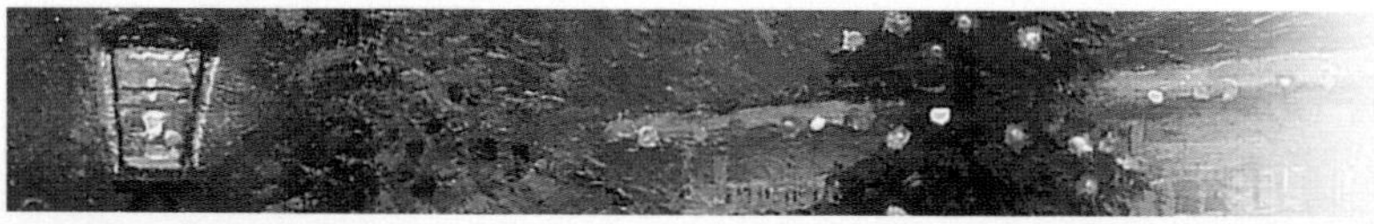

28
Christmas in July

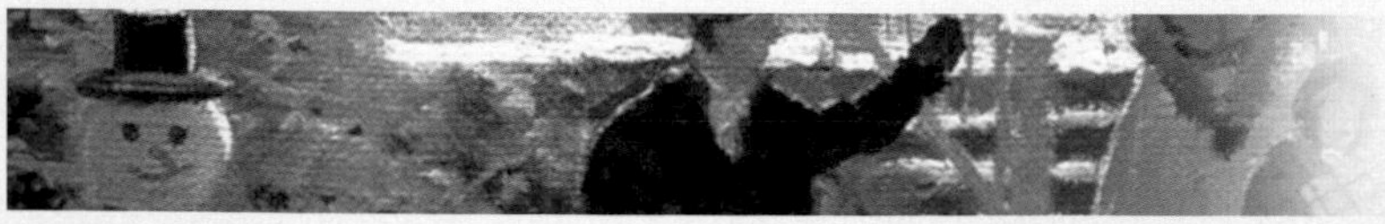

32
Serendipity

4

38
Small Sacrifices

44
Fears on a Silent Night

50
Gifts, Large and Small

56
Christmas Dawn

64
*The Sentinel
on Bedford Street*

72
The Christmas Touch

Thomas Kinkade

THE *Christmas Pool*

IMAGINE CHRISTMAS AS A POOL in the stream of time. The autumn current flows cold and clear, but as it rushes and chatters around a long November bend, it falls into deep December.

And slows down.

Or seems to.

Just beyond the pool, the stream hurries on, tumbling into rapids and racing into the channel of a new year. But at the pool, we may (if we wish it so) find a moment's quiet. Green in the long light of a winter afternoon, bottomless blue on a frosty morning, or mirroring the cold fire of stars in the stillness of a December night, the pool speaks of mysteries beyond our years and invites us to pause and ponder.

We don't have to hurry through Christmas.

With a little forethought, with a little discipline, we can make time to take time. We can stop running long enough to listen to the music, savor the lights, delight in the moment, remember the good days of seasons past, and think about enduring things—even as the stream of time glides on by.

There is always something timeless about Christmas.

Perhaps it's because of the way it came to us. On a given day, in a given place, at a given moment, Eternity entered into Time, permanently changing both. Timelessness intersected the temporal. Everlasting life—enduring light!—pierced a closed system of darkness and sorrow, rendering it closed no more forever. Heaven sent its best to earth, and He came to dwell among us. Into time, through time, and at the right time.

A birth. A Baby. A Boy. And then a Man.

Pondering Christmas won't give us any more time, but gazing into the depthless pool just might help time stand still, if only for a season. We might give ourselves to pursuits long overlooked in our preoccupation with deadlines, schedules, obligations, and incessant busyness.

Eternity entered into Time, permanently changing both.

Love of the season.

Love of family.

Love of neighbors and friends.

Love of strangers along the path.

And love of the One who came and gave so much more than we could begin to imagine.

THE Courts OF THE Lord

IN LATER YEARS, MY CHRISTMAS VISION would embrace scenes of snowy lanes and warm, cozy cottages with bright frosty windows and lazy wreaths of wood smoke rising from the chimneys.

In later years, I would fill my canvases with horse-drawn sleighs, festive ice-skaters in the park, church steeples piercing the winter twilight, and holiday gatherings in grand old Victorian homes with wide porches and horses tied at the hitch on the street.

In later years, my imagination would walk crowded, hometown sidewalks, peer through department store windows, and ponder the rosy tints of a deep winter sunset over a tiny English village.

But the Christmas of 1979 bore no resemblance to any such scene. It didn't look anything like a gilded greeting card or some magical depiction from Currier & Ives.

Yet it was the most remarkable Christmas of my life.

I was a young bachelor, living alone in a Pasadena ghetto known as the "Golden Palms."

Our little complex was surrounded by abandoned, graffiti-scarred buildings in a neighborhood populated by drug addicts, drunks, mentally challenged folks, and a smattering of poor but serious art students who didn't seem to notice or mind the run-down buildings or the trashy streets.

If you had hope in that place, it was because you carried your hope around with you—it was a cinch you wouldn't find it in that environment. The Golden Palms was anything but golden.

And yet that year, on that Christmas, it somehow was.

Golden.

Everything was. My mind was filled with golden thoughts; my mouth was filled with golden words; my spirit was filled with golden emotions.

Just a few months before, I had received Christ as my Savior, and the whole world was new. Even in a dreary, hopeless place, that Christmas I had hope—and the most profound sense of joy in my life I had ever experienced.

Some might dismiss my elation and wonder as nothing more than the typical experience of a new believer. But it was anything but typical for me. I found myself on a new frontier, like Lewis and Clark first setting eyes on the shimmer of the blue Pacific, and nothing looked the same to me.

It's not as though my lifestyle had radically changed, because at that time it hadn't. I was still the same complex bundle of weaknesses, sinful habits, old thought patterns, and distressful failings. My life wasn't what you'd call "cleaned up." Not then. Not yet.

But something was happening at my very core.

It was exhilarating and frightening and wonderful. The living Christ was there, and nothing could ever really be the same again. I felt myself possessed of a profound sense of faith and a power beyond anything in my experience.

I expected to hear God's voice at every turn.

I expected to sense His presence every waking minute.

I expected miracles every day.

I expected extraordinary things to happen at any moment.

Beyond all doubt, I knew I had a power in me—Thom Kinkade, unknown young artist—that could change the world. It had nothing to do with self-confidence and everything to do with a confidence in God, which seemed to grow by the hour. I knew that nothing in the world could oppose me or stand against me. Not now. Not ever.

I could say, with David, "For by You I can run against a troop, By my God I can leap over a wall" (Psalm 18:29, NKJV).

I was young, I was naive, and I didn't have much background in the faith or in knowledge of the Bible. Yet at the same time I had an overwhelming sense of the awesomeness of God, and the sure knowledge that He had chosen me and had plans for me beyond my comprehension.

What a Christmas that was!

I was as alone as I'd ever been in my life. I had no money. My mother had moved to Missouri, I didn't know where my dad was, and I had very little contact with my brother or sister. I didn't have a steady girlfriend. My dreams of succeeding as an artist seemed light-years from fulfillment. I lived in a depressing ghetto. I should have been lonely. I should have been down. But instead, I was filled with awe and joy. To think that I could walk right into the courts of the living God and speak to Him whenever I wanted! To think that His Holy Spirit—the eternal God, in all His fullness—chose to live in my dumpy little apartment with me. The Golden Palms were the very courts of the Lord.

It's a funny thing how the light burns even brighter, becomes even more precious, in the midst of darkness. The light of Christ is shining brightly in my home even now, but then, there is a lot of light in my home, and somehow it doesn't stand out as much. But in those days after I was first converted, the light was so bright it almost blinded me. I was living in a dark place, and I still had a lot of darkness in my own life—so the contrast was startling. It was so obvious what that light was because of all the darkness that surrounded me—human depravity on every side. The junkies. The perverts. The drunks. The weirdos. The strange women. The con artists.

I was just a small-town kid who wanted to be a painter and live some kind of bohemian lifestyle, like the famous artists in Paris I'd read about. I'm not sure I really knew what I was getting into. And now, looking back, I realize that I could have gotten mixed up with the wrong people or gotten into stuff that would have killed me. Only God's provision and protection kept me alive during that phase of my life.

I had an overwhelming sense of the awesomeness of God, and the sure knowledge that He had chosen me and had plans for me beyond my comprehension.

But on that first Christmas as a Christian, my surroundings didn't even matter. When you have Christ Himself inside you, what does it matter where you are or where you live?

For Christmas dinner, I probably popped into one of the little beaneries in my neighborhood. I probably sat on a stainless-steel stool and ate a greasy cheeseburger at the Clown Café, a junky all-night doughnut shop and grill filled with a tacky collection of clown artifacts and faded pictures of Red Skelton.

It might as well have been the Ritz-Carlton in New York City.

It might as well have been roast duckling in raspberry sauce, with cappuccino cheesecake for dessert.

It was Christmas, and Christ had come to earth. Only He wasn't a baby, and He wasn't in Bethlehem.

He was hanging out with Thomas Kinkade in the Golden Palms.

FIRST *Christmas*

OUR FIRST CHRISTMAS TOGETHER as a married couple came at a time when we were thinking about survival. We had very little money and just a few sticks of furniture, and we were still living in the slummy little Golden Palms apartment where Thom had lived as a bachelor.

I was working the night shift as an RN in a nearby hospital, and because he wanted to be with me, Thomas became a night painter, working on his gallery pieces through the night so that we could have "dinner" together at 7 A.M. and then sleep through the morning hours.

As Thom has already mentioned, the Golden Palms featured a colorful cast of characters in those days. We had a congenial acquaintance with obvious drug dealers, alcoholics, down-at-the-heel art students, and a ragtag collection of other longtime residents who were down on their luck or just couldn't afford anything better.

At least the owner of the complex, David Tong, had a sense of celebrating the season. Sometime in early December he would haul out a single string of multicolored lights and drape them along the railing of the second-floor apartments. A few of us would turn out for the lighting ceremony, when David would plug the string into one of the outdoor outlets, and voilà! Christmas in East L.A.!

On the Sunday before Christmas, Dell, one of the more flamboyant of our neighbors, would don a red Santa hat and hold a Christmas barbecue in the parking lot. So we would stand around munching hamburgers and hot dogs in the warm, smoggy southern California sunshine, and it didn't seem much at all like the old movies or the Christmases we had known as kids.

Even so, we were only newly launched on our marriage adventure, and we were having too much fun to worry about our poverty.

Beyond all of those things, this was the year Thomas gave me one of the best Christmas presents I have ever received in my life.

It was a little impressionistic painting of the two of us, walking hand in hand through a field in the moonlight. To this day, it occupies an honored place on our bedroom wall. Thomas had painted it right after one of our first dates, when I was a senior in high school and he was an art student at the University of California. He had come home to Placerville on a break from school, and we had gone on a long walk together, just talking and

> We were having
> too much fun
> to worry about
> our poverty.

laughing and catching up. Even though we had been friends since childhood, I think it became obvious to both of us that night that there could be something even more special ahead for us.

It had been a magical night, with love just beginning to dawn.

And now, on Christmas Day in the first year of our marriage, I was looking down at that little moonlight scene and remembering it all over again.

After dropping me off, he had gone home and stayed up half the night creating this

> *It had been a magical night, with love just beginning to dawn.*

perfect little painting. Even though he was only a beginning art student at the time, he was somehow able to completely capture that moment in faraway Placerville. In the painting, Thomas appears to be in thought, musing, looking down a little. And I'm looking straight out toward the horizon.

That's probably just the way it was.

Thomas, thoughtful, wondering about the future, as he held my hand and we walked through the dry, pine-fragrant air of a northern California night. And me, trusting, happy, spending an evening with a young man I had admired since I was barely out of pigtails and he was a thirteen-year-old paperboy.

Where had he hidden the painting? How had he kept the secret? I have trouble keeping a surprise to myself for two days, let alone for years. Somehow, Thomas had managed to tuck the little painting away among our meager possessions, and had saved it for this year, this Christmas, at our improbable, cramped little home at the Golden Palms.

We didn't have much money that year to decorate or go anywhere or eat a fancy holiday meal, but it was that gift that really touched my heart on our first Christmas.

HAPPY *Birthday* JESUS

I

IN OUR FAMILY, GETTING READY for Christmas is as exciting as the day itself.

Decorating our home is every bit as fun as opening the presents under the tree.

As you might expect in the home of the "painter of light," our house is filled with

Christmas lights—inside and out. Sweet-smelling candles flicker and shine in every corner,

and we keep our gas fire burning brightly over our pretend Yule logs. It takes me at least ten

minutes every morning to turn on all the lights and light all the candles. (You should see our

power bill in January!)

The girls and I like to keep busy in the kitchen making Christmas cookies and banana

bread to take to our neighbors—and maybe even some of our famous family-recipe fudge. The

girls get so wound up about planning what to get or make for each other, their mom, dad, and

grandparents. They dream up all kinds of wild ideas and schemes—crafts and gags and

projects, yummy things and fun things and totally silly things. As November yields to

December, a lot of whispering, giggling, and secret meetings seem to occupy diverse corners of our home. And that's what blesses me most: seeing my children so very thrilled about what they can give. This year Chandler surprised Thomas and me with a special story she had written, just for Christmas, just for us.

At different times during the season, we'll bundle ourselves into the car and take what we call our "light drive," cruising nearby neighborhoods to look at Christmas lights. Every time we see a home that's lit up, we call out, "Happy birthday, Jesus!" (We end up saying it quite a lot!) It's just one of the ways we remind ourselves what Christmas is really all about.

This has been a concern of ours since our firstborn, Merritt, was a baby. We wanted her—and all our children—to understand from their earliest days that Christmas is about celebrating and honoring Jesus Christ. When Merritt was still in diapers, we started a tradition of making a birthday cake on Christmas Eve, putting candles on it, and singing "Happy Birthday" to Jesus—then blowing out the candles. After all these years, we still do it. The cake. The candles. The singing. Christmas is still, first and foremost, a birthday party for the King.

Christmas is still, first and foremost, a birthday party for the King.

This may not go over well with everyone, but when Merritt was still little, we had to make a decision about how to handle Santa Claus. Of course, he's everywhere you look and everywhere you turn, and it's difficult to explain to a little one why we're not quite as excited about him as everyone else seems to be. We told Merritt that Christmas is a very, very big birthday party for Jesus—that's why there is a cake and candles—and that we give presents to each other out of our love for the Christ child. And Santa Claus? He's like the birthday clown who's there to help us with the party.

I personally imagine that St. Nicholas himself wouldn't mind this description. I think he would have loved to be a helper at any party for the true Lord of Christmas!

One of the first things we unpack in late November is a little manger made out of sticks and filled with straw. We set it on the table in the family room and just look at it for a while before we finish our unpacking and decorating. It seems so very, very empty. Then on Christmas morning, when the girls get out of bed, they run over to the manger. Sure enough, the baby Jesus has arrived. It's just a little baby doll, but the girls adore it and take turns holding it and carrying it around.

The girls have almost a month to think about what Christmas would be like if Jesus hadn't been born in that stable so long ago.

It's been a wonderful little touch to our family traditions. The girls have almost a month to think about what Christmas would be like if Jesus hadn't been born in that stable so long ago. The empty manger begs to be filled. That little bed of straw seems to long for the One it will cradle and hold. It reminds us that the Christmas season without Jesus is sad and empty and makes little sense at all.

But they know He is coming! As the days go by, they anticipate that little manger being filled. Then on Christmas morning there is the joy of welcome and adoration of the Little One who came so very far to be with us and to save us.

Christmas IN July

FOR SOME REASON, I've never been inclined toward painting wintry Christmas scenes when it's actually winter. Most of my deep winter visions and snowy hometown scenes were birthed as the warm summer sun splashed through my studio windows. And it hasn't been the aroma of cinnamon candles or Christmas cookies that filled the room as I painted those snowy country lands and cozy yuletide cottages; it's been the fragrance of flowering trees and freshly-mown lawns. Rather than listening to carols or Handel's *Messiah* as I painted, I'd be more likely to hear the sleepy drone of a honeybee in Nanette's fuchsias through my open window—or the squeals of my little girls playing in the sprinkler.

My Christmas paintings, you see, have little to do with the calendar. They grow out of Christmas daydreams. They spring from the longings in my heart.

I imagine that's true for most artists. Inspiration will grow either out of fond memories, or out of unmet needs and yearnings. That's the story, of course, behind my depictions of homey little cottages with lights shining in every window and smoke curling from the chimneys. As a boy from a broken family, that's the kind of home I ached for as I walked down the dirt lane toward our house after school. But our windows were always dark as I rounded the bend. Mom had to work long hours to support us, and the house and yard were scruffy and run-down because no one had the time or energy to put into them. So as the years went by and I began to paint for a living, the desires of my heart began to emerge from the canvas. In fact, they began to simply take over my paintings.

It wasn't long into my career before another latent boyhood dream began to find its way into my art. A white Christmas. When you grow up in California—even northern California, on the road to Tahoe—snow is a rare visitor on December 25. Placerville was a grand little town and a fun place to grow up, but I don't recall even one snowy Christmas. Being the child I was, however, I developed a very active fantasy life about what a white Christmas would look like on Main Street in Placerville. I was very literally "dreaming of a white Christmas," and I did it for years. I guess you could say I still do.

> *Christmas lives in my imagination and in my childhood longings.*

I wondered how it would look with snow drifting down around the streetlights...strings of colored lights casting their glow on frosty store windows...and the sound of holiday shoppers crunching through the frozen snow on the sidewalks.

Have you ever been homesick for a place you've never been? I imagined what it would be like to experience Christmas in some tiny village in the White Mountains of New Hampshire...or in a little rural valley in Vermont...or stopping by the woods on a snowy evening with Robert Frost—lovely, dark, and deep.

Christmas lives in my imagination and in my childhood longings. I love it when the season is finally here, and my four girls and I relish all the excitement and surprises, the lights and love, the flavors and fun. Christmas in December is one of the highlights of our whole year.

How wonderful that it happens all over again in the middle of July.

Serendipity

IT WASN'T REALLY CHRISTMAS. It was January.

Yet for Thom and me, with just a little bit of pretending, it became the white Christmas we'd never known.

We were back home living in Placerville, and for one crazy season, the snow forgot it was falling in California. It seemed like the big white flakes would never stop, drifting into high mounds, breaking tree branches, and knocking out power in our little town for four days.

With a good woodstove for heat and cooking, we did just fine. In fact, we did better than fine. It became a cherished memory. I had such fun cooking stews and beans and corn bread on the stove—in between nursing and caring for our first baby, Merritt.

For the first and only time in our marriage, Thom moved his easel and paints into the house. Without electricity, his studio was just too dark for painting. As it happened, the best-lit place in the house was the dining room, next to the kitchen, where there was plenty of southern light. Most artists prefer the softer northern light in their studios, but on those

34

dark, snowy days, the south light flooded our dining room and gave him enough light to paint.

Often, in the middle of winter, Thom's schedule will have him painting fragile spring flowers or a summer pathway winding alongside a stream. But that year, as he looked out our windows at our old hometown, so magically transformed by the rare snowfall, he painted dreamy snow scenes that I count among my favorites to this day.

When we needed a break, we'd strap on our cross-country skis, Thom would bundle up little Merritt in a backpack baby carrier, and we'd take off down our country lane. It was so pristine and beautiful. I know that people from North Dakota or northern Minnesota who read these words are probably thinking, What's the big deal? But for a little California family who'd never seen a white Christmas, snow in January would just have to do!

Today I have a backup power system in my studio. If we ever lost power, I'd be able to go on painting without much interruption. But in those days there were no backups. And painting was no pastime or leisure activity. It was our bread and butter, as it is to this day. We needed the income from selling those paintings—my little family was depending on me. I couldn't help but feel a little discouraged hauling all my gear out of the studio and trudging through the snow to the house. How could I concentrate? Would there be enough light? Would I be able to meet my deadlines? I had no idea that God was about to transform a setback into serendipity.

As the years go by, so many times and in so many ways I have learned that God will provide for us as we trust in Him—even when the times seem dark or difficult. In fact, many of our most memorable moments as a couple and a family have grown out of those times of hardship and struggle.

As it was, I set up my easel in our sunny dining room—which had windows on all sides, almost like a sunporch—and began my work.

Nanette became very domestic, bustling around the kitchen, singing happy little songs under her breath. All kinds of delicious odors began drifting from the woodstove. Little Merritt slept much of the time, and when she was awake, her baby chatter didn't really bother me.

I'll never forget those few days and the happiness of just being together as a little threesome while the snow fell and fell and fell.

It wasn't the Swiss Alps. It wasn't Vermont. It wasn't even Christmas.

It was Placerville in January, and that was just fine. The gift of memory will endure many long years after we've forgotten what was under the tree.

So many times and in so many ways I have learned that God will provide for us as we trust in Him.

Thomas
Kinkade

SMALL *Sacrifices*

SEVERAL YEARS AGO, Thomas, Merritt, Chandler, and I were invited to Washington, D.C., for the lighting of the national Christmas tree.

It was bitterly cold that year, and we were all dressed in long wool coats, scarves, mittens, and hats. In spite of the honor and fun of being part of that event, we thin-blooded Californians were just freezing in that icy wind.

We couldn't help but be relieved when the ceremony was over and our taxi pulled up to the curb. All four of us bundled inside. The girls and I snuggled in the backseat, and we began to feel cozy for the first time in a couple of hours.

Our route back to the hotel took us through some of the rougher streets in our nation's capital. Thom, who was riding in the front seat with the cabbie, suddenly noticed something ahead of us and got our attention. He pointed out a homeless man in a light shirt, huddled on a curb with his arms wrapped around his legs. We had already experienced the bite of that December wind—it must have easily had a subzero chill factor.

"Look at that poor man," Thom said, "out there in this freezing weather with no coat or blanket. He'll never make it through the night." Suddenly he asked the cabdriver to pull over for a moment. "I'll just be a second," he said.

We watched Thom get out of the car, kneel by the homeless man, whisper something in his ear—and then take off his coat and wrap it around the man's shoulders. Now coatless, he hurried back to the shelter of the cab.

"What did you say to him?" Chandler asked.

"I said, 'Jesus loves you.' Maybe he'll make it through the night now."

The next day, of course, Thomas had no coat. But it was bearable, since we weren't outside for very long and were on our way back to sunny California.

Sometimes, looking outward at Christmas can be as immediate as your own street or neighborhood.

The girls knew that their daddy wasn't suffering. They knew he could easily buy another coat anytime he wanted to. Even so, the incident made an impression. While the rest of us savored the warmth and snuggled together in the backseat, still glowing from the dazzle of ten thousand lights on a thirty-foot Christmas tree, Thom had noticed someone in danger—someone who needed immediate help. The girls were so touched to think that he would give away his brand-new coat to a street person he had never seen before.

We're trying to keep this sort of outward focus as a family—especially at Christmastime. The girls are always wanting to give special gifts and write notes to the World

Vision children we sponsor around the world. Just a few weeks ago, our church had a shoe drive for children in Russia, where the winters are so very cold and many families don't have money to buy quality shoes and boots. We got excited as a family as we all went to our closets and began gathering up as many shoes and boots and warm footwear as we could find to send to Russia. We could have just written a check, but it made it so much more personal for the girls to take their own shoes out of their own closets and put them in a box headed for girls their own ages in Russia. I think it helps them understand the love of God so much more when they actually picture another person they are helping with what they give.

Thomas and I are trying to give them opportunities to learn that our life here in California—in America—is not the way everybody in the world lives. Far from it. We have been incredibly privileged and blessed, and we need to foster a thankful and giving spirit.

Sometimes, looking outward at Christmas can be as immediate as your own street or neighborhood. This year we invited our neighbors, who aren't Christians, to dinner and then to our Christmas play at church. So much of the year, I have to admit, the Kinkades get self-absorbed, run at our own pace, stay insulated and safe behind our four walls, and forget that we even have neighbors. Christmas gives us that little extra prod to work harder at connecting with nearby families. We knock on a few doors up and down the street and try to bring our neighbors a festive little plate with homemade cookies and candy.

> *When you think back to Bethlehem, Christmas had very little to do with convenience... and everything to do with love.*

The other day I couldn't help noticing how excited our girls became about making gifts and getting in contact with our neighbors. They were really fired up, and the anticipation seemed to dance in their eyes. It made me just a little sad. It made me realize that they would like to give even more and make contact even more—not only at Christmastime, but all through the year. They don't lack the interest or the desire or the courage, just the opportunity, and that has to start with Thom and me.

It would mean some adjustments in our schedule.

It would mean some rethinking of our priorities.

It might mean sacrificing a little bit more of our "privateness" as a family, something we've increasingly cultivated and treasured as Thom's name has become more well-known around the world.

Even so, it may be the very thing we need to do.

When you think back to Bethlehem, Christmas had very little to do with convenience...and everything to do with love.

Fears ON A Silent Night

I THINK WE WOMEN HAVE A PERSPECTIVE on the story of Mary that no man (even an insightful and sensitive painter) can quite achieve. As a mother-to-be, carrying a child in your womb, you have such a sense of life being in God's hands—both your life and the life of your baby. It's all in God's control, because the amazing changes that happen to your body and emotions are so completely out of your control. When you finally cradle that new life in your arms, it's an overwhelming experience, coupled with an awesome sense of responsibility. As a Christian mother, looking into the face of each of my newborn girls, I have cried out to the Lord for His leading, His strength, and His guidance.

Then I think of Mary, a scared adolescent from the hill country who may have been no more than fourteen or fifteen years old. Without ever having known a man, she was pregnant by the Holy Spirit. And the child she carried was the Lord Himself, the Holy One of God, the Almighty.

Then, when her time had almost come and she was so heavy with child, she and her bridegroom had to journey to Bethlehem, with no guarantee of anywhere to stay or any kinswoman or midwife to help with her delivery.

Frightening as it must have been, in my view that was the easy part. How do you raise a child who is not only a child, but is also God? I feel so totally human and fallible in dealing with my own children. But what if your child was perfect? Would that be easy or difficult? I'm really not sure. I can't help but believe that you would continually be seeing your own sinful humanness in the light of that little one's perfection.

Even so, I see in Mary a woman who was willing to step back from her own dreams and plans and allow God to work through her life—to the very limit! She walked in such humble submission to God that her reply to the angel's announcement came naturally from her lips: "I am the Lord's servant.... May it be to me as you have said" (Luke 1:38).

> *I see in Mary a woman who was willing to step back from her own dreams and plans and allow God to work through her life— to the very limit!*

What trust! What simple, childlike faith. Did she realize what she was getting into? Maybe not—until Simeon's prophecy in the temple, when the old man looked her in the eyes and said, "This child is destined to cause the falling and rising of many in Israel, and to be a sign that will be spoken against, so that the thoughts of many hearts will be revealed. And a sword will pierce your own soul too" (Luke 2:34–35).

It's such a lesson to me, and one I pray I'll be able to teach my daughters. When you trust the Lord with all your heart and stay open to His leading, you may find yourself in situations and places beyond your dreams. Yes, there may certainly be pain, difficulty, and hardship, but you will be walking in the very heartbeat of His plans and purpose...and there is no better place to be than that.

No matter what.

❧ ❧ ❧ ❧ ❧ ❧ ❧ ❧ ❧ ❧

I have to wonder how much of the Lord's purpose in their lives Joseph and Mary actually grasped early on. We tend to hyperspiritualize the men and women in Scripture—draw halos around their heads and assume they were cut from a whole different bolt of cloth than you and me.

But in the end, they were just people.

Joseph was just a man, and Mary was just a teenage girl. Yes, they experienced angelic visitations and received messages from heaven. But put yourself in their place. Imagine you had such a dream or vision late one Sunday night. How would you feel about it Monday morning when you're back in the routine? How would it add up a week or two weeks later? Honestly now, would it seem like reality to you—or some kind of crazy dream?

I'm going to become pregnant—and I'm still a virgin?

My fiancée is with child—and she's been sexually pure?

How do those things look in the gray light of Monday morning, when you're sipping your coffee and rubbing the sleep from your eyes? Now skip ahead nine months and imagine you're Joseph, leading your young, very pregnant wife along on a donkey toward your hometown. It's the worst time to travel, and the roads are choked with traffic. But you have no choice. When Rome calls, you go. Your wife may very well give birth before you can even get to Bethlehem. And who will be there to help? Anyone at all? Will you—a simple carpenter with callused hands— actually have to deliver a baby? What if you do something wrong? What if she doesn't survive? What if you're out on the road somewhere with no shelter? What if bandits or rogue soldiers are lingering nearby? What if you get to an inn and you can't afford the room rate? What if you run into problems at the tax booth and end up owing more than you anticipated? Will there be enough money for food on the trip home—maybe with a little baby?

I personally believe that the "saintliness" of many of the Bible's heroes is just so much mythology. I think they were regular people, formed from the same common clay as you and me, who found themselves faced with both bewildering challenges and astounding opportunities. And some of them, like Joseph, responded in simple faith and obedience. But I still have to believe his stomach must've been knotted up with the pressure of those incredibly tense circumstances.

> They were regular people, formed from the same common clay as you and me, who found themselves faced with both bewildering challenges and astounding opportunities.

It's the same with Mary. Even though she's been deified by millions over the millennia—or portrayed as some superhuman, all-wise saint by Renaissance painters— I think people miss the point. She was vulnerable. She was fragile. She was frail. She was probably scared. And so very, very human.

Yet it is this very frailty and weakness that speaks so profoundly. It allows stumbling, failing people like us to dare hope that God might use us to accomplish mighty, even eternal, purposes.

OLDE
Porterfield
GIFT
SHOPPE

Thomas
Kinkade

GIFTS, *Large* AND *Small*

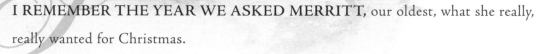

I REMEMBER THE YEAR WE ASKED MERRITT, our oldest, what she really, really wanted for Christmas.

Her answer took me aback a little.

She said she wanted a ball.

A ball? Yes. That was it. She asked for a simple playground ball, which cost maybe five or ten dollars. I'm sure she received numerous other things that year, but what a great time we had with that ball! There was no assembly required, no batteries, no warning labels, and no college course required to operate it. You just took it out of the box and headed outside to have fun.

Parents are wise, I think, to remember the simple things. If you're going to buy the newest and most elaborate toy the kids are begging for because they've seen it on TV, remember that it may very well be broken or cast aside in a day or two. And then it will be time for crayons. Or Legos. Or a doll. Or a ball.

We've been blessed with children who seem appreciative of everything they get. Perhaps because they're girls, they seem particularly excited about clothing—even the little ones. It was interesting to me to hear the yearning in our little five-year-old Evie's voice when she asked her mom about knee-high socks.

Age five has to be one of the more materialistic, me-me-me, bring-on-the-toys phases of life. But for Evie, knee-high socks represented a sort of rite of passage. Sometime last fall she had seen her older sister heading out the door for school wearing such an outfit—a white blouse, crisp skirt, and those wonderful knee-high socks. She looked down at her own little cotton top, pink corduroys, anklet socks, and red Keds tennis shoes, and she felt light-years away from such feminine sophistication. Don't forget that when you're five, seven years old seems an eternity away. Never mind that her oldest sister was already into the glamorous teenage world of nylons, makeup, and leg-shaving. When you're five, you see a seven-year-old in a skirt and knee-high socks as the ultimate in chic and womanliness.

Parents are wise, I think, to remember the simple things.

Sometime later in the day, Evie came to Nanette with eyes full of longing and a wistful softness in her little voice. "Mom," she said, "when am I going to be old enough for knee-highs?"

53

THE MANY LOVES OF CHRISTMAS

She might as well have been asking, "When will I be old enough to drive?" or "When will I be old enough to go to the prom?" I don't think she really expected anything to happen on the knee-high front for many long, weary years. Not until she was seven...or fifty.

Then came Christmas.

And a soft little package just for Evie.

A pretty fold of bright wrapping paper concealing...knee-highs! Her very own cream-colored knee-high socks.

Her joy was almost too radiant to behold. You would have thought we'd just bought her the entire inventory at Toys 'R' Us. She simply could not believe her eyes. It still amazes me to think about how a kid could get so wildly excited over a pair of socks. (I used to get socks, too, from one of my aunts, and it never did a thing for me.)

But for Evie, of course, it was more than a pair of socks.

She had arrived. She was now part of an exclusive sorority of urbane and classy womanhood.

She immediately put on the knee-highs, and I think she's worn them ever since.

For boys, of course, receiving socks at Christmas is next to an insult or a cruel joke. In fact, everything I desire my kids to model at this time of year is the opposite of how my brother and I viewed the big day. We were typical kids of the early sixties, growing up on TV, with cartoons that advertised every possible new toy and gadget. We were classic materialistic boys whose only concern was "How much are you going to give me this year? I need at least twelve hundred toys." Our Mom didn't have much money, but bless her heart, she did her best.

One year, when Patrick was in fourth grade and I was in fifth, she went all-out and bought us a Ping-Pong table. Pat and I were already pretty hot stuff with Ping-Pong: I was the Ping-Pong champ at my school and my brother first runner-up. So Mom bought us this outrageously big Ping-Pong table and did her best to keep it a surprise.

Fat chance!

How do you hide a Ping-Pong table? She tried. She really did. But about the best plan she could come up with was to fold it up in her bedroom and throw some blankets over it. We found it right away, of course, and worked mightily at feigning ignorance.

One day in early December, I was home sick and Pat came bounding in the door for lunch. On a whim I said, "Hey, let's get out the Ping-Pong table." So we rolled the thing out of Mom's room, unfolded it in the living

Her joy was almost too radiant to behold.... and she simply could not believe her eyes.

room, and soon had a fierce volley going. Wouldn't you know that this day of all days Mom decided to come home for lunch? We heard her car tires crunching in the gravel driveway, flew into a great panic, and started madly trying to fold the table.

Just as we were scrambling to push it into her room, she walked in and doubled over with laughter. Most likely she knew all along that she couldn't hide such a thing from two inquisitive boys.

Mom may not have had much help in making Christmas special for us or many resources to spend on our insatiable desire for the latest stuff. But we never lacked for fun.

And she never insulted us by gift wrapping underwear or socks.

Christmas Dawn

Nevertheless, there will be no more gloom for those who were in distress....
But in the future he will honor Galilee of the Gentiles, by the way of the sea,
along the Jordan—

The people walking in darkness
have seen a great light;
on those living in the land of the shadow of death
a light has dawned.
(Isaiah 9:1–2)

THESE VERSES OF SCRIPTURE, written thousands of years before Christ's birth, seem to refer to His first coming...when He walked along the Sea of Galilee, teaching and healing the people...when He sat on the banks of the Jordan with His disciples. In those days, people who had been walking in spiritual darkness for so many centuries, people who had been suffering under the oppression of the Romans, saw a Great Light. God's own Son walked among them, reaching out to those under the shadow of death.

Christmas reminds us of that coming—that bright and wonderful Light Who came into the world to save us and lift us out of darkness and despair.

Our world needs that light just as much today. This year. This Christmas. Many all around us are walking in darkness, with no idea where to turn or how to find a little peace and happiness in their lives. We rub shoulders with such men and women every day—in the aisles of the grocery store, in the neighborhood, at work, at school. How will they see the Great Light that is the Lord Jesus?

The answer, I think, is that He wants to shine through us. The Holy Spirit living in us is the light of Jesus. And I believe His light shines brightest in our love. People around us see Him not so much in our Christmas lights, yard displays, or fancy wreaths and decorations, but in our kindness, compassion, forgiveness, patience, and that unconditional love that goes so far beyond our own abilities or strength.

That's what I want my neighbors to see. For that matter, that's what I want my husband and children to see in my life. And no matter how efficient I may be in all my decorating and baking and buying presents and sending cards and Christmas letters, if I've missed letting His love shine through me, then I've really missed it all.

Christmas reminds us of... that bright and wonderful Light Who came into the world to save us and lift us out of darkness and despair.

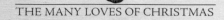

There's nothing wrong with all the celebrations and traditions, with Santa Claus and reindeer and Christmas parties and fun—we enjoy many such things as a family. The only danger is in getting so caught up in or preoccupied by all these external activities that the Holy Spirit has no room or opportunity to work through us—no chance to shine the light of Christ's love on those who have such empty, lonely, hungry hearts. And that describes people everywhere!

If I'm too busy or frazzled to take time for my children's concerns or my husband's needs, if I'm too wrapped up in personal cares or pursuits to offer someone in my path a big smile, a nonjudgmental listening ear, a hug, or a sincere "How are you?" then I've missed the most precious Christmas opportunity. Christmas has become, then, just what the rest of the cynical world calls it—"the holidays," and nothing more.

Lately my eyes have been open to how many deeply needy people I bump into every day. If you scratch just a little bit below the small-talk surface, you'll find people with problems and hurts that are approaching desperation.

> *If you scratch just a little bit below the small-talk surface, you'll find people with problems and hurts that are approaching desperation.*

Christmas gives us the opportunity to reach out to people in a special way. There is an openness and tenderness that just doesn't seem to be there at other times of the year. We have a brief window of time when we might step into their lives and become at least a small reflection of the Great Light who stepped into our world two thousand years ago.

The people who walk in darkness will see a great light—a light that will shine on all who live in the land where death casts its shadow.
(Isaiah 9:2, NLT)

Think of the prophet Isaiah, peering thousands of years into the future. A succession of awesome and bewildering images passes before his eyes. Perhaps some of the scenes are misty, out of focus. It's difficult to tell whether he's looking at events soon to take place, thousands of years ahead, or at some impossibly distant point in an unimaginable future.

But one thing he knows for sure.

There is a vast and blanketing darkness. And that darkness is pierced by a mighty light—a light so radiant it throws back the shadow of death itself.

What was that light?

A star that guided men from the east? Some cosmic phenomenon that tugged at the minds and souls of scholars, who packed their camels and set off across the world to investigate?

That may have been part of it. But the rest of Isaiah 9 reveals that the light was more than a light. The light was a Person.

> *For a child is born to us, a son is given to us.*
> *And the government will rest on his shoulders.*
> *These will be his royal titles:*
> *Wonderful Counselor, Mighty God,*
> *Everlasting Father, Prince of Peace.*
> (Isaiah 9:6, NLT)

The Great Light was the Son of God, Almighty Creator, Who left heaven, humbled Himself to become a tiny embryo in a teenager's womb...and was born on the first Christmas night long ago.

Isaiah saw that. Did he see even more? Are we, too, part of that radiance that floods the stubborn darkness—we who have Christ living within us in these shadowed and uncertain days?

Jesus said to His disciples: "You are the light of the world. A city on a hill cannot be hidden.... Let your light shine before men, that they may see your good deeds and praise your Father in heaven" (Matthew 5:14, 16).

In these unsettled and unsettling times, in these days when the mention of the word *Jesus* in public is considered in bad taste and Nativity scenes in front yards and town squares are regarded as politically incorrect (and possibly illegal), we have the opportunity to let His life shine through ours. Our world, too, is one "where death casts its shadow." In every city and town, in every neighborhood, in every school and workplace, there are those who sorrow, who walk the cliff edge of despair.

Our world today needs to see the Great Light. In just the last few weeks, Nanette and I have rubbed shoulders with a number of people who, because of the tragedies and seemingly impossible circumstances in their lives, have all but lost hope. They are living, as the Scripture says, "in the land where death casts its shadow." As we seek to step into their lives with comfort, hope, and friendship, we become an inseparable part of the Light that startled sleepy shepherds and shook kings on their thrones on the first Christmas. *Wonderful Counselor, Mighty God, Everlasting Father, Prince of Peace.*

Who knows what Isaiah saw when the Lord allowed the millennia to part like gauze curtains and the prophet to gaze upon wonders yet to be. He may have been looking at Bethlehem on that night when the sky was torn from one end to the other and heaven's light flooded the hills of Judea.

But he may also have been seeing the reflection of Christ in those small acts of love and sacrifice that you perform this very day.

CHRISTMAS
OPEN
HOUSE

THE *Sentinel* ON *Bedford* STREET

OF COURSE I'M A ROMANTIC—I wouldn't dream of denying it. So discount my words, if you will, but I still maintain that there is something in the air at this time of year. Something that can't be explained by the frantic merchandising and runaway consumerism that begins the week after Halloween. Something that can't be written off as the musings of an idealistic painter with his head in the clouds.

Christmas is the season of light, which speaks so profoundly to the deepest part of our Christian experience. Despite all the attempts to remove Jesus from the day created expressly to honor Him, I definitely detect a sense of God's Spirit permeating the land.

It's something I've noticed since childhood—and I know it's more than my admittedly active imagination. There is a spring in the step, a smile on the face, and a greater sense of people enjoying one another.

I can hear some of my readers saying, "Goodness. It's obvious he hasn't done much Christmas shopping in the malls lately." It's true. I do avoid those settings as much as I can.

66

(With a wife and four daughters, the Kinkades are usually well represented in that venue without my help.) But I'm still optimistic that underneath the thin veneer of a false and cynical secular "holiday," True Christmas still sends forth its timeless fragrance and honest joy.

As November rolls into December, nobody notices the changes in town like a paperboy—except for the postman. As I would pedal my Stingray bike around the hilly streets and gravel lanes of Placerville, delivering folded copies of the *Mountain Democrat*, I would notice the subtle changes as the big day approached. A wreath on a door. A string of those big colored lights everyone used to use. Some cutout paper snowflakes on a living-room window. New and amazing window displays at the Ben Franklin five-and-dime and Arayan's department store.

But there was nothing subtle about Big John O'Malley's house up on Mosquito Road. It was a jaw-dropping wonder, and that's just the way he wanted it.

There's a John O'Malley in every town, I suppose. The local businessman and sometime-politician who always manages to slap more backs and grab more than his share of attention at high-school ball games, community picnics, and fireworks displays. Not to mention all the ink in the local newspaper.

The O'Malley family—Big John, his wife, and his two daughters—were all very large people. What's the politically correct designation these days? People of size? For whatever reason, the two O'Malley girls had a fondness for buzzing around town on two tiny Honda trail bikes. It was quite a picture. You couldn't miss them—coming or going—and I'll admit to stopping my bike and just staring as they went by.

But a day or two after Thanksgiving, it was the O'Malley's house that came into the limelight. Every day that I rode by, the wonder grew. In all my life, I'd never seen so many colored lights in one locality. Lights on the eaves, lights around the windows, lights on the porch, lights on the chimney, lights on the trees and bushes and hedges. (I think they would have put lights on their dog—or at least reindeer antlers—if he would've sat still for it.) In addition, Big John had turned his yard and rooftop into an animated menagerie. There were illuminated plastic Santa Clauses, reindeer, elves, snowmen, and candy canes, topped off by a "Peace on Earth" sign spelled out in blinking lights.

It was so amazingly tacky and over-the-top that it had a certain charm. People would drive from as far away as Pollock Pines or Shingle Springs to stop and stare. For those few weeks, Mosquito Road became Tinseltown.

Placerville's downtown celebration was considerably more understated than Big John's tourist attraction up on the hill. Yet it meant more to me.

There was an old, lightning-scarred redwood on Bedford Street by the post office, just across the street from the courthouse and the Pacific Gas and Electric Company building. Somehow it had escaped the saw and the ax when the town was founded back in the Gold Rush of '49. It always seemed kind of dignified to me, all by itself downtown, separated by miles from its fellow redwoods. It reminded me of a lonely old man who had outlived all his contemporaries and now stood alone in the winter wind.

It reminded me of a lonely old man who had outlived all his contemporaries and now stood alone in the winter wind.

For who knows how long, the redwood had been designated the official Placerville Christmas tree.

On the first Sunday of each December, Mom would take us downtown for the lighting ceremony. For all its age and dignity, the redwood had seen better days. Lightning strikes had topped the tree and lopped off some of its big limbs. Just a few gnarly old branches were left, but the town fathers built a skirt of wires, hung with lights and emanating out from somewhere up on the trunk, to give it the semblance of a traditional Christmas tree.

It wasn't the most symmetrical or artistically beautiful display you've ever seen, but everyone knew that the tree had been there years before we came along, and most of us felt it had a certain unspoken right to participate in the festivities.

In my imagination, the tree reminded me of Christmases long ago and far away, out of time, out of memory...something old beyond our brief lifespan...something solemn and joyful all at the same time...something with ancient roots, deep below the surface of modern transitory changes.

Imagine walking to the town square, late on a wild and windy December night, and standing alone before that tree. Imagine the wind in those old branches, thick as the trunks of young pines. Imagine the colored lights moving and swaying in the wind. Old and new, entwined. Wires and electric cords screwed into the venerable trunk. Electric reds and blues, greens and yellows, overlaying ancient boughs and starlight.

Big John O'Malley had the most lights and the biggest show in town every Christmas, but my heart belonged to the lonely old redwood on Bedford Street.

All the flash and sparkle and tinsel are just fine...just so long as there is something old and true and alive underneath.

THE *Christmas Touch*

IT STRUCK ME THE OTHER DAY that there is just a little bit of Christmas in every one of my paintings.

It doesn't matter if it's a tranquil summer setting in the English countryside, a Victorian garden on a misty morning, a thatched-roof cottage on a cobblestone lane, the rain-washed streets of New York's Fifth Avenue, or a grand stone manor basking in the soft light of some autumn evening lost in time...there is Christmas in every one of them.

Through the years, many people have told me that they've noticed Nanette's initials showing up in various hidden places in a painting. Or maybe someone will catch on to the fact that I've painted Nanette and yours truly somewhere within a crowd of pedestrians in a busy town square.

I've always enjoyed adding those occasional whimsical touches to my artwork, but I will tell you with all sincerity that the Christmas touch is infinitely more important to me than any of those things.

74

If you look in one of the lower corners of my paintings, you will see my signature—and below that, a little fish symbol accompanied by the tiny words *John 3:16*. That's a Bible passage, of course, that has been familiar and precious to many generations of believers:

> "For God so loved the world that he gave his one and only Son, that whoever believes in him shall not perish but have eternal life."

We might be hearing a lot about the Virgin Mary, the shepherds, and the magi at this time of year, but I believe the twenty-six words of this brief passage to be the greatest Christmas verse—and the most profound message—of all.

I began adding the "John 3:16" touch to my paintings from the earliest days. For me, it's something more than a logo or some rote repetition or indifferent tradition. It's the center of my very life. The core of all that I am. My paintings are nothing more than an extension of God's love and grace to me. Whether we choose to acknowledge it or not, all of our gifts and talents are wrapped up in a package of His incomparable love for each one of us.

My paintings are nothing more than an extension of God's love and grace to me.

That's where True Christmas starts, of course.

With God's love.

John 3:16 begins where everything begins, with the reaching, yearning, risk-taking, incalculably costly love of our Creator. He could have kept that love to Himself, safe, eternally protected, and perfectly fulfilled within the celestial realms of heaven and the imponderable mysteries of the Trinity.

But He didn't.

Because He loved, He gave.

And that's the message of Christmas.

> *He gave the very best He had—His one and only Son, the delight of His heart.*

He did not keep His love "safety sealed" somewhere in the great beyond. He gave the very best He had—His one and only Son, the delight of His heart. He gave Him to be born in the poverty, cruelty, and violence of first-century Roman Palestine. He left Him in the care of a young Jewish girl and a good-hearted, if slightly bewildered, itinerant carpenter. It was a land of prejudice and simmering hatred. It was an era of brutality and oppression under the heel of a power-mad Roman Caesar and a cruel puppet king in Jerusalem.

Why did He give such a gift...and leave it in such a place?

The reason is right in the verse. He did it so that "whoever believes" in Jesus (don't you love that beautiful word *whoever?*) will not have to face a second death, an eternal separation from the life and light and joy of God's presence, but will come into possession of eternal life on the other side of that final curtain.

There could be no greater Giver. There could no greater Gift. And there certainly could be no greater need.

Any Christmas gift that has ever been given—whether by sultan, king, or billionaire, no matter how expensive and elaborate, no matter how creative, thoughtful, or imaginative—pales before this staggering gift of God's own Son.

From my earliest days as a paperboy in Placerville, California, God gave me the yearning and desire to create works of art. Then, when I was a teenager, He brought mentors into my world who patiently taught and instructed me—not only in painting techniques, but also in the art of life. He sent me to art school, protected me through lean and hungry times and long days of wandering, led me to salvation in Jesus, and brought a wise and lovely woman to my side as my life partner. He has been pleased to bless the works of my hands as they've spread across the world.

And it's all a gift. It's all grace. It's all from Him. That's why I put that little Christian symbol and *John 3:16* on every painting. It's a declaration that all I have and all I do is because of Him.

For me, Christmas will always be something more than a solitary square on December's calendar. My whole life has changed because "God so loved...that He gave." That little fish and that tiny Scripture reference right alongside my signature is meant to remind me—or anyone who cares to notice—that Christmas is with me always. And His name is Jesus.

1991

Thomas
Kinkade

ART INDEX

COPYRIGHT:
Evening Glow

INTRODUCTION:
Deer Creek Cottage

CHAPTER ONE:
Victorian Christmas IV

CHAPTER TWO:
Victorian Christmas III

CHAPTER THREE:
Victorian Christmas II

CHAPTER FOUR:
Christmas Memories

CHAPTER FIVE:
Home for the Holidays

CHAPTER SIX:
Village Christmas

CHAPTER SEVEN:
Silent Night

CHAPTER EIGHT:
Old Porterfield Gift Shoppe

CHAPTER NINE:
Moonlit Village

CHAPTER TEN:
Victorian Christmas

CHAPTER ELEVEN:
Sunday Evening Sleigh Ride

CLOSING IMAGE:
Christmas Eve